A Gift From

The Carter Family

Reptiles Rule

Triassic Life

Dougal Dixon

An Hachette Company

First published in the United States by
New Forest Press, an imprint of Octopus Publishing Group Ltd

www.octopusbook.usa.com

Published by arrangement with Black Rabbit Books

PO Box 784, Mankato, MN 56002

Dixon, Dougal.
Reptiles Rule : Triassic Life / by Dougal Dixon.
p. cm. -- (Awesome Ancient Animals)
Summary: "Describes some of the animals of the Triassic Period, a
time when reptiles were common and when the first dinosaurs, and
the ancestors of the mammals, started to evolve. Includes an Animal
Families glossary, prehistory timeline, and pronunciation guides"--
Provided by publisher.
Includes index.
ISBN 978-1-84898-629-9 (hardcover, library bound)
1. Paleontology--Triassic--Juvenile literature. 2. Animals, Fossil--
Juvenile literature. I. Title.
QE732.D59 2013
560'.1762--dc23
2012002750

Printed and bound in the USA

15 14 13 12 11 1 2 3 4 5

Publisher: Tim Cook Editor: Margaret Parrish Designer: Steve West

Contents

Introduction

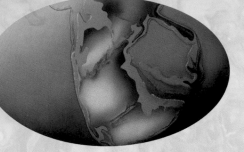

This map shows how the Earth looked in the Triassic Period. All of the continents were grouped into one mass of land.

This map shows how the Earth looks today. See how different it is! The continents have split up and moved around.

Awesome Ancient Animals follows the evolution of animals.

The Earth's history is divided into eras, which are divided into periods. These last millions of years. *Reptiles Rule* takes you back to the Triassic Period, when reptiles were common in the seas, the sky, and on the land. This is when the first dinosaurs, and the ancestors of the mammals, started to evolve.

A LOOK BACK IN TIME

This timeline shows how simple creatures evolved into many differnt and complex life-forms. This took millions and millions of years. In the chart, MYA stands for million years ago.

	BOOK	PERIOD	
CENOZOIC ERA	**THE ICE AGE**	1.81 MYA to now QUATERNARY	This is a time of Ice Ages and mammals. Our direct relatives, Homo sapiens, appear.
	ANCIENT MAMMALS	65 to 1.81 MYA TERTIARY	Giant mammals and huge, hunting birds rule. Our first human relatives start to evolve.
MESOZOIC ERA	**CRETACEOUS LIFE**	145 to 65 MYA CRETACEOUS	Huge dinosaurs evolve. They die out by the end of this period.
	JURASSIC LIFE	200 to 145 MYA JURASSIC	Large and small dinosaurs and flying creatures develop.
	TRIASSIC LIFE	250 to 200 MYA TRIASSIC	The "Age of Dinosaurs" begins. Early mammals live alongside them.
PALEOZOIC ERA	**EARLY LIFE**	299 to 250 MYA PERMIAN	Sail-backed reptiles start to appear.
		359 to 299 MYA CARBONIFEROUS	The first reptiles appear and tropical forests develop.
		416 to 359 MYA DEVONIAN	Bony fish evolve. Trees and insects come on the scene.
		444 to 416 MYA SILURIAN	Fish with jaws develop and sea animals start living on land.
		488 to 444 MYA ORDOVICIAN	Primitive fish, trilobites, shellfish, and plants evolve.
		542 to 488 MYA CAMBRIAN	First animals with skeletons appear.

Psephoderma

By the Triassic Period, many animals lived on land, although some had returned to the seas. The placodonts were reptiles that lived in the ocean and ate shellfish. *Psephoderma* had a long, pointed snout and strong jaws. It was ideally adapted for picking shellfish off reefs and crushing them with its broad teeth.

Psephoderma

Their armored backs protected the placodonts from other sea-dwelling reptiles—some of which were much bigger and fiercer.

Placochelys

Psephoderma had a shell and looked a little like a turtle, although it was not closely related. It evolved a similar shape and shell because it had a similar lifestyle.

Henodus

Animal fact file

NAME: PSEPHODERMA (ROUGH SKIN)

PRONOUNCED: SEF-OH-DER-MA

GROUP: PLACODONTS— A GROUP OF SWIMMING SHELLFISH-EATERS

WHERE IT LIVED: THE SEAS AROUND SOUTHERN EUROPE

WHEN IT LIVED: LATE TRIASSIC PERIOD (228 TO 200 MILLION YEARS AGO)

LENGTH: 5 FT (1.5 M)

SPECIAL FEATURES: TURTLELIKE SHELL ON THE BACK, AND ANOTHER OVER THE HIPS

FOOD: SHELLFISH

MAIN ENEMY: OTHER BIG SWIMMING REPTILES AND SHARKLIKE FISH

DID YOU KNOW?: NOT ALL PLACODONTS HAD SHELLS. SOME LOOKED LIKE GIANT NEWTS. ONE RELATIVE, PLACODUS, WAS 6 FT 6 IN (2 M) LONG.

Nothosaurus

Nothosaurus was one of the earliest sea-dwelling reptilian hunters. Its feet were webbed, like those of a seal, and it had a long neck and toothy jaws— perfect for snatching at fish. *Nothosaurus* spent most of its time in the water, although it had to come to the surface to breathe.

There were several types of nothosaur. *Lariosaurus* was one of the smallest, at 24 in (60 cm) long. *Ceresiosaurus* and *Nothosaurus* were bigger and better adapted to life in the sea. They used their feet like paddles.

Ceresiosaurus

8

Nothosaur fossils have been found all over the world. *Nothosaurus* was the most common and widespread nothosaur.

Lariosaurus

Nothosaurus

Animal fact file

NAME: NOTHOSAURUS (FALSE LIZARD)

PRONOUNCED: NOTH-OH-SORE-US

GROUP: NOTHOSAURS

WHERE IT LIVED: FROM EUROPE AND NORTH AFRICA TO CHINA

WHEN IT LIVED: THE WHOLE OF THE TRIASSIC PERIOD (250 TO 200 MILLION YEARS AGO)

LENGTH: 10 FT (3 M)

SPECIAL FEATURES: WEBBED FEET AND LONG SHARP TEETH

FOOD: FISH AND SMALL REPTILES

MAIN ENEMY: SHARKS

DID YOU KNOW?: ITS LEG BONES SHOW THAT NOTHOSAURUS WAS ABLE TO CLAMBER AROUND ON LAND. IT CAME ASHORE TO LAY ITS EGGS.

Shonisaurus

Among the reptiles that returned to the sea, the most famous are probably the *Ichthyosaurs*—the "fish-lizards." They were fully adapted to life at sea and could not have survived on land. Some of the earliest, like *Shonisaurus*, were enormous—truly whale-sized.

Shonisaurus was the biggest sea animal of the Triassic. One species, *Shonisaurus* sikanniensis, was 69 ft (21 m) long. Its fossil was found in a remote riverbank in Canada.

Animal fact file

NAME: SHONISAURUS (LIZARD FROM THE SHOSHONE MOUNTAINS, NEVADA)

PRONOUNCED: SHON-EE-SORE-US

GROUP: ICHTHYOSAURS—THE FISH-LIZARDS

WHERE IT LIVED: THE OCEAN THAT COVERED PARTS OF THE UNITED STATES AND CANADA IN THE TRIASSIC PERIOD

WHEN IT LIVED: LATE TRIASSIC PERIOD (228 TO 200 MILLION YEARS AGO)

LENGTH: 50 FT (15 M)

SPECIAL FEATURES: ITS SIZE! IT WAS THE BIGGEST ICHTHYOSAUR KNOWN

FOOD: FISH AND INVERTEBRATES

MAIN ENEMY: NONE

DID YOU KNOW?: SCIENTISTS THINK THAT SHONISAURUS ONLY HAD TEETH WHEN IT WAS YOUNG. ADULTS WERE TOOTHLESS.

Their streamlined bodies enabled these reptiles to slide effortlessly through the water. The large paddles were fingers that had joined together.

Eudimorphodon

By the end of the Triassic Period some reptiles had mastered the skill of flying. Before then, a few lizardlike reptiles existed that could glide for long distances. The pterosaurs were reptiles that could fly by flapping their wings like birds. *Eudimorphodon* was one of the first to appear.

Eudimorphodon used its pointed front teeth to catch fish as it flew low over the surface of quiet lagoons. Its small back teeth held prey firmly in its grip.

Eudimorphodon had wings that were supported by a single, long fourth finger. Its tail helped it steer.

Animal fact file

NAME: EUDIMORPHODON (WITH TWO VERY DIFFERENTLY SHAPED TEETH)

PRONOUNCED: YOU-DEE-MORF-OH-DON

GROUP: PTEROSAURS—FLYING REPTILES

WHERE IT LIVED: ITALY

WHEN IT LIVED: LATE TRIASSIC PERIOD (228 TO 200 MILLION YEARS AGO)

BODY LENGTH: 2 FT (60 CM)

WINGSPAN: 3 FT (1 M)

SPECIAL FEATURES: TWO DIFFERENT TYPES OF TEETH

FOOD: FISH

MAIN ENEMY: BIG FISH AND BIG REPTILES

DID YOU KNOW?: THE FOSSIL OF A CLOSE RELATIVE, PREONDACTYLUS, WAS FOUND AS A BUNDLE OF BONES COUGHED UP BY A FISH THAT HAD EATEN IT OVER 200 MILLION YEARS AGO.

Desmatosuchus

Before dinosaurs, the largest land animals were relatives of today's crocodiles. Some of them, like *Desmatosuchus*, were actually plant-eaters. They fed on ferns and vegetation found near the oases of the desert landscapes of the time.

Desmatosuchus had weak, blunt teeth and a short snout. It held its head close to the ground, where the vegetation grew.

Desmatosuchus was covered in rows of armor plates. Spikes that curved outward from the shoulders and neck helped protect it against predators such as the meat-eating rauisuchians.

Animal fact file

NAME: DESMATOSUCHUS (LINK CROCODILE)

PRONOUNCED: DEZ-MATT-OH-SOO-KUSS

GROUP: AETOSAURS—A GROUP OF PLANT-EATING CROCODILES

WHERE IT LIVED: ARIZONA, TEXAS

WHEN IT LIVED: LATE TRIASSIC PERIOD (228 TO 217 MILLION YEARS AGO)

LENGTH: 16 FT (4.8 M)

SPECIAL FEATURES: LONG SPINES ON THE SHOULDERS USED FOR PROTECTION

FOOD: LOW-GROWING PLANTS

MAIN ENEMY: CARNIVOROUS LAND-DWELLING RAUISUCHIANS

DID YOU KNOW?: DESMATOSUCHUS WAS A VERY EARLY MEMBER OF THE PLANT-EATING AEFOSAURS.

Arizonasaurus

The fiercest meat-eaters in Triassic times were big land-dwelling rauisuchians like *Arizonasaurus*, relatives of crocodiles. They did not crawl like modern crocodiles, but walked on straight legs, like dogs. They hunted big plant-eating reptiles that lived in the oases of the time.

Arizonasaurus probably used its sail to take in heat from the sun on chilly mornings. This would have made it more active than its slow-moving prey and helped it to hunt.

Arizonasaurus fossils were first found in 1947, but they were thought to be dinosaur bones. In 2000, scientists realized the fossils came from a rauisuchian. The new animal was named *Arizonasaurus*.

Animal fact file

NAME: ARIZONASAURUS (LIZARD FROM ARIZONA)

PRONOUNCED: AH-RIH-ZONE-UH-SORE-US

GROUP: RAUISUCHIANS—A GROUP OF LAND-DWELLING CROCODILES

WHERE IT LIVED: ARIZONA

WHEN IT LIVED: MIDDLE TRIASSIC PERIOD (245 TO 228 MILLION YEARS AGO)

LENGTH: 10 FT (3 M)

SPECIAL FEATURES: TALL SAIL

FOOD: PLANT-EATING REPTILES

MAIN ENEMY: NONE

DID YOU KNOW?: ARIZONASAURUS LOOKED LIKE DIMETRODON, AN EARLIER REPTILE WITH A SAIL. THE TWO REPTILES ARE NOT CLOSELY RELATED. THEY LOOK THE SAME BECAUSE THEIR LIFESTYLES WERE SIMILAR.

Eoraptor

In the Late Triassic, many big land animals were relatives of crocodiles and other reptiles. The first dinosaurs were very small. *Eoraptor* was only the size of a turkey, but it was an ancestor of the huge, magnificent dinosaurs to come.

Although *Eoraptor* was not very big, it was very active and fierce. It hunted small creatures of the time, such as reptiles and insects.

Eoraptor had long jaws and sharp teeth, like those of later meat-eating dinosaurs. Like later predators, it had strong hind legs, a long, flexible neck, and grasping fingers. A heavy tail helped it balance.

Animal fact file

NAME: EORAPTOR (EARLY HUNTER)

PRONOUNCED: EE-OH-RAP-TER

GROUP: THEROPOD DINOSAURS

WHERE IT LIVED: PATAGONIA IN SOUTH AMERICA

WHEN IT LIVED: LATE TRIASSIC PERIOD (228 MILLION YEARS AGO)

LENGTH: 3 FT (1 M)

SPECIAL FEATURES: THE EARLIEST DINOSAUR KNOWN

FOOD: SMALL ANIMALS AND INSECTS

MAIN ENEMY: BIG LAND-DWELLING RAUISUCHIANS

DID YOU KNOW?: LATER MEAT-EATING DINOSAURS HAD THREE, OR EVEN TWO, FINGERS. LIKE ITS ANCESTORS, EORAPTOR STILL HAD FIVE, ALTHOUGH TWO OF THEM WERE TINY. CHANGES LIKE THIS HELP SCIENTISTS TRACE THE EVOLUTION OF DINOSAURS.

Unaysaurus

Dinosaurs quickly evolved into two groups: meat-eaters and plant-eaters. Unaysaurus was one of the earliest plant-eaters. Like other dinosaurs of the time, Unaysaurus was smaller than many other animals around. Its descendants were much bigger—they were the massive, long-necked sauropods such as *Brachiosaurus*.

Unaysaurus had serrated teeth. It ate plants that grew on the ground and probably stood on its hind legs to reach leaves in the trees.

Part of a *Unaysaurus* skeleton was found in Brazil in 2004. Its hind legs were longer and heavier than its front legs. This suggests that it spent a lot of time standing.

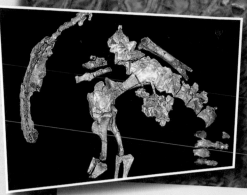

Animal fact file

NAME: UNAYSAURUS (BLACK WATER LIZARD, NAMED AFTER THE AREA WHERE IT WAS FOUND)

PRONOUNCED: OO-NAY-SORE-US

GROUP: PROSAUROPOD DINOSAURS

WHERE IT LIVED: BRAZIL

WHEN IT LIVED: LATE TRIASSIC PERIOD (228 TO 200 MILLION YEARS AGO)

LENGTH: 8 FT (2.4 M)

SPECIAL FEATURES: THE EARLIEST KNOWN OF THE LONG-NECKED PLANT-EATERS

FOOD: LEAVES AND FERNS

MAIN ENEMY: BIG LAND-DWELLING CROCODILES AND EARLY DINOSAURS

DID YOU KNOW?: UNAYSAURUS IS CLOSELY RELATED TO DINOSAURS FOUND IN NORTH AMERICA, GERMANY, AND CHINA.

Antetonitrus

Antetonitrus was one of the first sauropods, a group of huge, long-necked plant-eaters. The sauropods evolved from primitive prosauropods in the late Triassic Period. *Antetonitrus* looked like the bigger prosauropods. We can tell it was not the same by the different arrangement of bones in its feet.

Some trees of the late Triassic Period had tough, swordlike leaves. These provided defense against new plant-eaters like *Antetonitrus*.

Later dinosaurs like *Camarasaurus* (pictured) looked similar to *Antetonitrus*. *Camarasaurus* used its large toe claw to defend itself against predators.

Animal fact file

NAME: ANTETONITRUS (BEFORE THE THUNDER— THE LATER SAUROPODS ARE SOMETIMES CALLED THE "THUNDER LIZARDS")

PRONOUNCED: ANT-EE-TONE-ITE-RUS

GROUP: SAUROPOD DINOSAURS

WHERE IT LIVED: SOUTH AFRICA

WHEN IT LIVED: LATE TRIASSIC PERIOD (215 MILLION YEARS AGO)

LENGTH: 26 TO 30 FT (8 TO 10 M)

SPECIAL FEATURES: THE EARLIEST KNOWN SAUROPOD

FOOD: LEAVES AND TWIGS

MAIN ENEMY: MEAT-EATING DINOSAURS AND LAND-LIVING CROCODILES

DID YOU KNOW?: WHEN SCIENTISTS FIRST DUG UP ANTETONITRUS THEY THOUGHT IT WAS A PROSAUROPOD. NO ONE REALIZED IT WAS A COMPLETELY NEW DINOSAUR UNTIL 20 YEARS LATER.

Coelophysis

The early meat-eating dinosaurs were small, but many made up for this in cunning. For instance, *Coelophysis* hunted in packs. Pack-hunting animals can successfully hunt beasts much larger than themselves.

Coelophysis was probably a scavenger as well as a hunter and ate what it could find. Many types of fish and reptile have been found in its stomach.

Two forms of *Coelophysis* fossil have been found. The thinner, more delicate one is thought to be the female.

Animal fact file

NAME: COELOPHYSIS (HOLLOW FORM)

PRONOUNCED: SEE-LOW-FYE-SIS

GROUP: THEROPOD DINOSAURS

WHERE IT LIVED: ARIZONA AND NEW MEXICO

WHEN IT LIVED: LATE TRIASSIC PERIOD (228 TO 216 MILLION YEARS AGO)

LENGTH: 10 FT (3 M)—MOSTLY NECK AND TAIL; ITS BODY WAS ABOUT THE SIZE OF A FOX

SPECIAL FEATURES: LIVED AND HUNTED IN PACKS

FOOD: OTHER REPTILES

MAIN ENEMY: BIG LAND-DWELLING RAUISUCHIANS

DID YOU KNOW?: A FOSSIL SKULL OF COELOPHYSIS WAS TAKEN ON THE SPACE SHUTTLE *ENDEAVOUR* IN 1998. IT WAS THE FIRST DINOSAUR IN SPACE!

Liliensternus

By the end of the Triassic Period, some of the dinosaurs were quite large. *Liliensternus* was one of the first big hunters. It was big enough to hunt and eat the earliest of the long-necked plant-eaters.

Two *Liliensternus* dinosaurs attack a prosauropod. They had two head crests that ran from the nostrils to behind the eyes. These were used to signal one another.

In 1802, footprints were found in some Triassic rocks in Connecticut. They were thought to have been made by giant birds. However, after the discovery of fossils, such as this *Liliensternus*, it was realized that they were the footprints of meat-eating dinosaurs.

Animal fact file

NAME: LILIENSTERNUS (FROM HUGO RUELE VON LILIENSTERN – AN EARLY PALAEONTOLOGIST WHO ORIGINALLY DISCOVERED THE FOSSILS)

PRONOUNCED: LIL-EE-EN-STER-NUS

GROUP: THEROPOD DINOSAURS

WHERE IT LIVED: GERMANY, FRANCE

WHEN IT LIVED: LATE TRIASSIC PERIOD (225 TO 213 MILLION YEARS AGO)

LENGTH: 20 FEET (6 METERS)

FEATURES: LARGE MEAT-EATER WITH TWO CRESTS ON THE HEAD

FOOD: OTHER DINOSAURS

MAIN ENEMY: NONE

DID YOU KNOW?: LILIENSTERNUS MAY HAVE PREYED ON LARGER DINOSAURS THAT WERE STUCK IN QUICKSAND.

Cynognathus

One group of reptile became very similar to mammals in the Triassic Period. They were probably warm-blooded, like mammals, and had a similar body shape. They may have even had fur. This group eventually evolved into the mammals themselves. *Cynognathus* was one of the most mammal-like of these reptiles.

Scientists think *Cynognathus* had fur because the bones of its snout show tiny pits where whiskers would have been.

The skull of the *Cynognathus* is similar to the skull of a mammal. Only the jaw shows that it was a reptile.

Animal fact file

NAME: CYNOGNATHUS (DOG JAW)

PRONOUNCED: SY-NOG-NAY-THUS

GROUP: THERAPSID GROUP OF MAMMAL-LIKE REPTILES

WHERE IT LIVED: SOUTH AFRICA

WHEN IT LIVED: MIDDLE TRIASSIC PERIOD (245 TO 230 MILLION YEARS AGO)

LENGTH: 5 FEET (1.5 METERS)

FEATURES: TEETH LIKE A DOG, WITH NIPPING INCISORS AT THE FRONT, STABBING CANINES AT THE SIDE, AND MEAT-SHEARING MOLARS AT THE BACK

FOOD: OTHER ANIMALS

MAIN ENEMY: THE BIG LAND-LIVING CROCODILES

DID YOU KNOW?: THE JAWBONE OF CYNOGNATHUS, OR SOMETHING CLOSELY RELATED, HAS BEEN FOUND IN ANTARCTICA. THIS SHOWS THAT AFRICA AND ANTARCTICA WERE JOINTED TOGETHER IN TRIASSIC TIMES.

Animal Families Glossary

Aetosaurs—a group of plant-eating reptiles, very closely related to the crocodiles. They were covered in armor and lived on land in the Triassic Period.

Ichthyosaurs—the group of seagoing reptiles that were so well-adapted to living in the sea that they looked like dolphins or sharks, with fins on the tail and back and paddles for limbs. They were common in the Triassic and the Jurassic periods but died out in the Cretaceous.

Nothosaurs—sea reptiles that had long jaws for catching fish, and webbed feet for swimming through water. Several kinds of nothosaur lived in the shallow waters around Europe and Asia in the Triassic Period.

Placodonts—a group of swimming reptiles that fed on shellfish. Many had shells like turtles, although they were not related.

Prosauropods—an early dinosaur group; they were plant-eaters and had long necks for reaching into trees. They were the biggest animals of the Triassic and early Jurassic, but not as big as their descendants—the sauropods.

Pterosaurs—the flying reptiles of the age of dinosaurs. They had broad leathery wings supported on a long fourth finger and were covered in hair to keep them warm.

Rauisuchians—a group of land-dwelling meat-eaters of the Triassic Period, closely related to the crocodiles. They were the fiercest animals of the time.

Sauropods—the plant-eating dinosaur group that had huge bodies, long necks, and long tails. They were the biggest land-dwelling animals that ever lived and reached their peak in late Jurassic times.

Therapsids—the most mammal-like group of the mammal-like reptiles. They were covered in fur and had teeth like the teeth of a mammal. Some were so mammal-like that you would think they were dogs.

Theropods—the meat-eating dinosaur group. They all had the same shape—long jaws with sharp teeth, long strong hind legs, smaller front legs with clawed hands, and a small body balanced by a long tail.

Glossary

Adapted—changing to survive in a particular habitat or weather conditions.

Canines—strong, pointed teeth.

Carnivore—an animal that eats meat.

Cunning—clever at using special resources to reach a desired goal.

Dinosaur—large group of meat-eating or plant-eating reptiles that no longer exists.

Evolution—changes or developments that happen to all forms of life over millions of years as a result of changes in the environment.

Evolve—to change or develop through time.

Fossil—the remains of a prehistoric plant or animal that has been buried for a long time and become hardened in rock.

Incisor—sharp-edged front tooth in the upper and lower jaws.

Lagoon—a shallow pond joined to seas or lakes.

Molars—special teeth used for grinding food.

Oases—green areas in a desert, where there is water and where plants grow.

Predator—an animal that hunts and kills other animals for food.

Primitive—a very early stage in the development of a group of plants or animals.

Prosauropod—late Triassic Period ancestors of long-necked, plant-eating dinosaurs.

Reef—a ridge of rock, sand, or coral near the surface of the ocean.

Reptile—a cold-blooded, crawling, or creeping animal with a backbone.

Reptilian—animals that look like a reptile.

Serrated—having a jagged edge like a saw.

Snout—an animal's nose.

Species—a group of animals that all look like each other.

Streamlined—an animal with a smooth, bullet-shaped body that allows it to move through air or water easily and quickly.

Trilobites—early type of sea animal that no longer exists.

Warm-blooded—animals, such as small mammals, that always have the same body temperature.

Index

Picture credits

Main illustrations: 18-19 Lisa Alderson; 6-7, 8-9, 10-11 Simon Mendez;
22-23, 24-25, 26-27, 28-29 Luis Rey; 12-13, 14-15, 16-17, 20-21 Chris Tomlin 4TL,
4TR, 5 (Cenozoic Era), 6, 9, 11, 13, 14, 18, 21, 25, 26, 29 Ticktock Media archive; 5
(Mesozoic Era top, Paleozoic Era top) Simon Mendez; 5 (Mesozoic Era center, Paleozoic
Era bottom) Luis Rey; 5 (Mesozoic Era bottom) Lisa Alderson; 17 Chris Tomlin; 23 Phil
Degginger/Carnegie Museum/Alamy

Every effort has been made to trace the copyright holders and we apologize in advance for any
unintentional omissions. We would be pleased to insert the appropriate acknowledgment in any
subsequent edition of this publication.